Life in the
dark

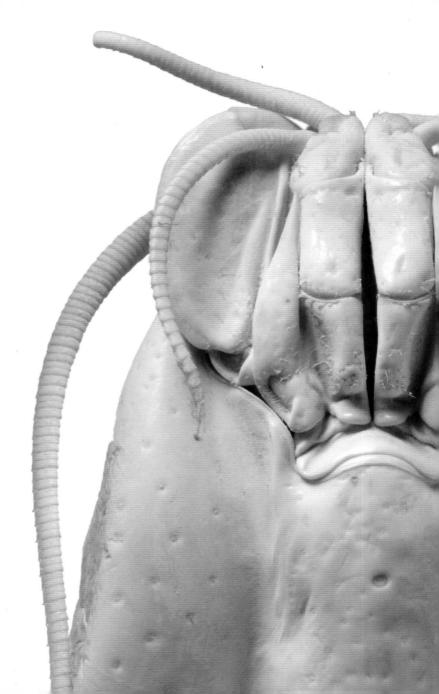

This page:
Blind vent shrimp,
Rimicaris kairei,
see p.69

Previous page:
Oryba sphinx moth,
Oryba kadeni, see p.9

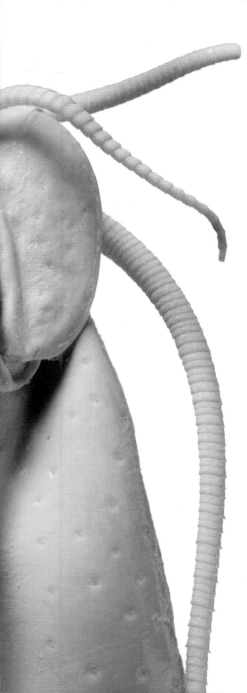

Leave the sunlight behind and venture into the dark. Travel to places where moths dance in the moonlight, bats dangle in caves and strange sea creatures lurk in the ocean depths. Enter these worlds and come face-to-face with the creatures that live there. Discover their stories, feel their surroundings and explore their lives.

This is life in the dark.

Life at night

As the last light of the day fades, under the cover of darkness, foxes emerge from hiding, badgers sniff out tasty meals and frogs serenade potential mates. From cities to countryside, jungles to deserts, creatures of the night are thriving.

Nocturnal creatures emerge and venture into the darkness to forage, hunt and find a mate. They rely not only on their sense of hearing, touch and smell but also on their sense of sight. We struggle to see clearly but in the dark many nocturnal animals have excellent night vision. Their eyes are adapted to make the most of the light from the Moon, stars, streetlights and buildings. In the limited light some creatures have evolved to see in detail but only in black-and-white, whereas others have adapted to see coloured but blurry images.

The night is far from silent! From serenades to alarm calls, an entire chorus of noises erupts after dark. Sounds travel differently at night – the cooler air temperatures carry soundwaves more slowly and towards the ground so they can be heard from further away. Calls, croaks and songs help animals to find each other as they search for a mate. But making sound can be dangerous. Supersensitive ears detect the tiniest scuttles and the quietest of squeaks, helping predators home in on their prey. Those under threat must rely on their sharp hearing and quick reactions to evade the talons, teeth and beaks of their attackers.

Touch is a key sense for us in the dark – entering a dark room, we reach out feeling for the light switch. Many nocturnal animals also rely on their sense of touch, supplementing their vision or hearing with what they can feel to help them move through the night with ease. Highly sensitive whiskers and bristles pick up tiny movements in the air, enabling animals to catch a passing insect or sense a predator nearby.

The night air is filled with smells. In the pursuit of a tasty meal, nocturnal animals use their noses to smell food deep in the soil or to sniff out an individual tree within a forest. Their noses have adapted to detect particles in the night air over huge distances, enabling them not only to track down food but to smell each other.

It is not just noses that are used for smelling. Insects use their antennae to detect natural chemical perfumes called pheromones released by the opposite sex. Night-flying moths produce pheromones to communicate and to find each other in the dark. The scent drifts through the night air signalling to other moths and attracting potential mates. Some male moths have bristles called hair pencils under their wings that help to fan and disperse the pheromones they make in the glands beneath the bristles. The feathery, super-sized antennae of many male moths have thousands of tiny sensory hairs that help to sense a female's pheromones. Astonishingly, some moths can smell each other from up to 10 kilometres away.

Most bats actually see well in the dark but they often use echolocation and other senses to find food and to navigate at night. They make a range of clicks and squeaks too high pitched for us to hear. These clicks bounce off trees, insects and animals and return like echoes, helping the bat to work out what and where something is in the dark. But not all bats have it their own way.

Although flying at night allows moths to avoid day-time predators such as birds, it does mean that they become tasty targets for bats. But moths have evolved a defence mechanism – noise. Some moths are able to make a rapid series of clicking noises using a structure on the side of their bodies called a tymbal organ. When merged together these clicks sound like a screech. Producing this screech at the right moment can confuse a bat's echolocation signal or scare it away, providing the moth with an opportunity to escape.

The arrival of the morning Sun poses a challenge. After a busy night nocturnal animals need to find a safe place to rest, hiding inside dens or burrows until the darkness returns. Others have evolved cryptic camouflage that allows them to hide in plain sight from day-time predators. Some even have adaptions that protect their eyes from the strength of the Sun's rays, so they can keep an eye out for predators or continue feeding during the day.

For most of us the night-time is for sleeping, but for many animals the night is not only full of opportunities but also a way to avoid the perils of day-time living. For some it's a way to hide from predators, for others it's an opportunity to hunt, and for those living in deserts they can avoid the heat of the scorching Sun. But with increasing night-time human activity, the night is becoming lighter and noisier than ever before, impacting the lives of nocturnal animals around the world.

Human-made light pollution at night is increasing by two per cent globally each year. This increase in nocturnal light is changing the way both day-time and night-time animals around the world hunt, feed, mate, stay safe and interact with each other. Some day-time animals have started to take advantage of the extra light to hunt and forage at night, whereas many nocturnal animals, which depend on the darkness to survive, are beginning to struggle as light levels increase.

TAWNY OWL
Strix aluco
Europe and the Middle East

Tawny owls have large tube-shaped eyes that allow them to see brighter images at night by making the most of any moonlight. This means they can fly through the forest in the dark without bumping into branches as they hunt.

OWL MONKEY
Aotus trivirgatus
Northern Amazon Basin

This is the only nocturnal species of monkey in the world. Its eyes are larger and rounder than those of monkeys that are active in the day, which means they absorb more light. This allows the owl monkey to see shapes and detail in the dark.

NET-CASTING SPIDER
Deinopis sp.
Southern hemisphere

This net-casting species has the largest eyes of any spider. Its eyes are 2,000 times more sensitive than our eyes, enabling it to spot prey at night. Waiting for passing insects, it dangles from branches and then pounces with its springy net.

ORYBA SPHINX MOTH
Oryba kadeni
Central America and northern South America

The oryba sphinx moth's eyes are extremely large and so are able to take advantage of any available light. Their brain also processes what they see more slowly, which helps the moth see more detail in the dark.

EUROPEAN MOLE CRICKET
Gryllotalpa gryllotalpa
Europe

Male mole crickets sing at night to attract females. They dig a small burrow that is perfectly shaped to tune a harmonious sound and reflect it upwards. When a female hears a song she likes, she drops down into the burrow to mate.

KAKAPO
Strigops habroptilus
New Zealand

The kakapo has a unique
night-time mating ritual. Males
dig a bowl-shaped hollow in
the ground, sit in it and make
low-pitched booming noises to
attract females. The shape of
the burrow amplifies the sound,
which can travel up to one
kilometre.

TAWNY FROGMOUTH
Podargus strigoides
Australia

Look closely at the bristles around the frogmouth's unusual beak. It is thought that these tiny bristles help it to feel the movement of air created by the wings of flying insects – its favourite food.

STAR-NOSED MOLE
Condylura cristata
North America

Can you see this mole's unusual
star-shaped nose? It has 22
feelers covered in thousands
of sensors. By pressing its nose
against the soil the mole feels
for earthworms and builds a
picture of its surroundings.

HAZEL DORMOUSE
Muscardinus avellanarius
Europe

Dormice twitch and scoop their whiskers in a unique movement known as whisking. They use their whiskers to sense their surroundings and to judge distances, helping them to find food and scamper through the trees at night.

PALE-THROATED SLOTH
Bradypus tridactylus
Brazil and Venezuela

Sloths are active at night, as well as during the day. Moving from branch to branch, they use their sense of smell to detect living branches containing sap so they can avoid dead branches that might break.

LARGE FLYING FOX
Pteropus vampyrus
**Malaysia, the Philippines
and Indonesia**

The largest bat in the world,
the flying fox, uses its nose to
sniff out nectar and fruit in the
dark. At night it searches for
its favourite foods – mangos,
bananas and the flowers of
coconut trees – in the forest.

LITTLE SPOTTED KIWI
Apteryx owenii
New Zealand

Unusually for a bird, this kiwi's nostrils are at the tip of its beak. The kiwi pokes its nostrils into the leaf litter and down into the soil to sniff out insects and earthworms. The flightless kiwi is vulnerable to predators, so forages at night to avoid being seen.

OWEN's KIWI.
APTERYX OWENI.
South Island, New Zealand.

KOALA
Phascolarctos cinereus
Australia

Koalas spend most of the day asleep, usually waking at night to feed. Eucalyptus leaves make up 95 per cent of their diet. Most koalas have a favourite eucalyptus tree that they eat from, which they are able to sniff out amongst the others in the forest.

**MALE ANCHEMOLA SPHINX
MOTH (underside and upperside)**
Eumorpha anchemolus
**Central America and
South America**

The male sphinx moth
produces a lemony scented
pheromone to signal to a
female that it is the same
species and is ready to mate.

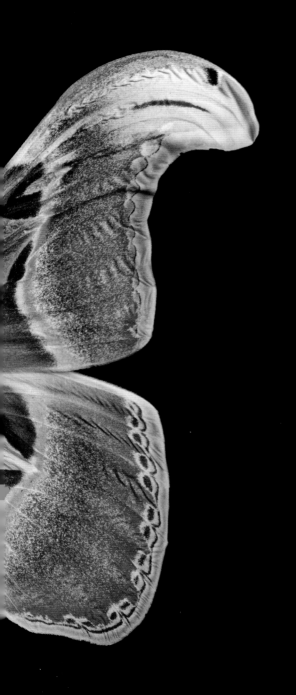

FEMALE ATLAS MOTH
Attacus atlas
Southeast Asia

Female atlas moths produce a scent to attract males to mate with. Sometimes the scent is so strong that male moths gather around a cocoon before the female has even hatched.

TAWNY FROGMOUTH
Podargus strigoides
Australia

COMMON POTOO
Nyctibius griseus
Northern South America

EUROPEAN NIGHTJAR
Caprimulgus europaeus
Europe to eastern Asia

These three nocturnal birds come from different parts of the world, but they all look very similar. Their feathers provide camouflage to keep them hidden from day-time predators. During the day the potoo and frogmouth sleep in trees while the nightjar rests on the forest floor.

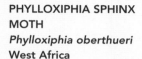

PHYLLOXIPHIA SPHINX MOTH
Phylloxiphia oberthueri
West Africa

VERDANT HAWK MOTH
Euchloron megaera
Africa and Madagascar

It isn't just nocturnal birds that blend into the background to stay safe during the day. Imagine you're in a forest, would you be able to spot these moths sitting completely still among the leaves?

WHITE-LINED GECKO,
Gekko vittatus
Indonesia

This gecko's large eyes are highly sensitive and detect colour, helping it to see more clearly at night. During the day it shrinks its pupils to wavy slits so it can keep watch for predators while protecting its eyes from the sunlight.

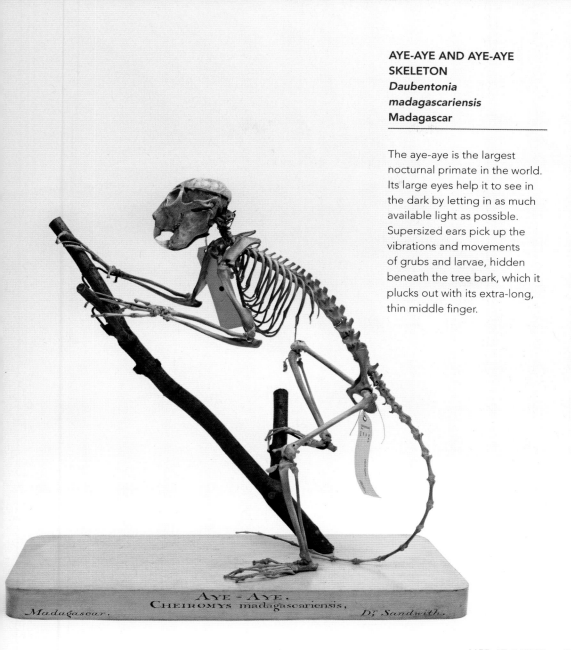

AYE-AYE AND AYE-AYE SKELETON
Daubentonia madagascariensis
Madagascar

The aye-aye is the largest nocturnal primate in the world. Its large eyes help it to see in the dark by letting in as much available light as possible. Supersized ears pick up the vibrations and movements of grubs and larvae, hidden beneath the tree bark, which it plucks out with its extra-long, thin middle finger.

AYE - AYE.
CHEIROMYS madagascariensis,
Madagascar.   Dr Sandwith.

EASTERN SPINY MOUSE
Acomys dimidiatus
The Middle East

Look at the eastern spiny mouse's pale coat. It blends in well with the sand at night, disguising the mouse from predators as it forages for seeds, insects and grasses to eat.

ROWLAND WARD LTO. 166 PICCADILLY W

EURASIAN STONE CURLEW
Burhinus oedicnemus
**North Africa, Europe
and Asia**

While most other birds are
sleeping, the stone curlew is
feasting on the many insects,
slugs and worms that come out
at night. Can you see its large
eyes? These help the curlew to
find its dinner in the dark.

GIANT ANTEATER
Myrmecophaga tridactyla
Northern South America

The giant anteater's good sense of smell means it can forage for ants at night as well as during the day. Anteaters sometimes eat after dark to avoid the heat of the Sun, but might also be feeding during the night-time near towns in order to avoid people.

DUNG BEETLE
Scarabaeus satyrus
Africa

These beetles scavenge dung,
roll it into a ball and then bury
it as food for their young. To
navigate in a straight line and
escape from their competitors
as quickly as possible, dung
beetles follow the faint path
of light of the Milky Way in the
sky above.

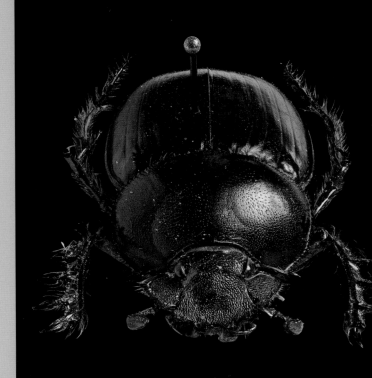

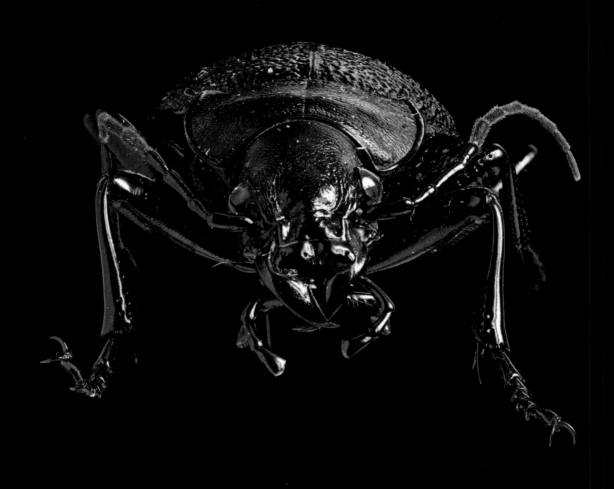

NIGHT-ACTIVE CARABIDAE BEETLE
Carabus coriaceus
Europe

DAY-ACTIVE CARABIDAE BEETLE
Carabus lafossei
Asia

Both of these beetles have adapted to protect themselves from the heat of the Sun. The night-active beetle comes out at night to avoid the Sun altogether – being black helps to camouflage it from nocturnal predators. Whereas the day-active beetle's metallic colour reflects sunlight keeping it cool during the day.

MANX SHEARWATER
Puffinus puffinus
**Atlantic Ocean and Skomer
in Wales**

While Manx shearwaters are
well adapted to life at sea,
they are very clumsy on land,
making them easy targets
for large gulls waiting on the
shore. To avoid being attacked,
they return to their burrows to
feed their chicks only under the
cover of darkness.

PEREGRINE FALCON
Falco peregrinus
Worldwide

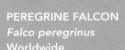

The peregrine falcon usually hunts during the day, but due to increases in night-time urban light in some cities it has been able to start hunting at night. This is bad news for nocturnal birds that now have a new predator to deal with.

BOAT-BILLED HERON
Cochlearius cochlearius
Central America and northern South American

Scientists don't know why these nocturnal herons never fish when there is a significant amount of light around. Both moonlight and human-made light disturbs them. Increases in night-time light pollution could mean that these herons struggle to feed.

GREATER HORSESHOE BAT
Rhinolophus ferrumequinum
Europe, the Middle East, eastern China and Japan

Unlike most species, horseshoe bats use their noses rather than their mouths to echolocate. The horseshoe-shaped folds of skin around their noses focus and sharpen the echolocation beams so the bats can hunt prey more accurately.

GREATER BULLDOG BAT
Noctilio leporinus
**Central America and
South America**

Known as the fishing bat, the
greater bulldog bat can detect
the movement of jumping fish
and the ripples of water they
make using echolocation. They
swoop down to catch fish out
of the water with their long,
sharp claws.

MALE LUNA MOTH
Actias luna
North America

Look closely at the tails on
the wings of this moth – can
you see a twist in them? This
delicate twist reflects sound
in an unexpected direction
so that an echolocating bat is
unable to pinpoint the position
of the moth.

Life in
caves

Leave the outside world behind and dare to enter the mouth of the cave. Hiding in this rocky underworld, creatures lie in wait, listening for echoes and feeling for the tiniest of movements. Deeper down life survives in an underground world of total darkness.

From craggy ceilings to flooded caverns, caves can make a good home for all sorts of animals. The temperature inside is stable and life here is sheltered from the weather outside. The dark, rocky crevices offer plenty of places for animals to conceal themselves from predators. Animals here make the most of the food available – whether that's hunting other cave-dwellers or feeding on their poo. But caves can be challenging environments. Over time creatures have evolved to catch prey, avoid predators and find their way in the dark.

How do you find your dinner in the dark? Some cave snakes, like the Puerto Rican cave boa, hunt by sensing the body heat of their prey. When we lose heat from our bodies we are actually emitting infra-red. Snakes have special detectors called pit organs that allow them to see infra-red light. So although the snake cannot see a bat in detail in the dark, it can see its outline from the heat it is giving off and go in for the kill.

Beyond the cave mouth, dark passages extend for many kilometres into the Earth. What could possibly survive down here? There's only one way to find out and that's to go cave diving, but this can be risky and, in some cases, even deadly. These deep chambers are dangerous places for us – the air trapped inside can be toxic, their passages are often flooded and it is pitch black. Divers need specialist equipment to be able to see, breathe, map their routes and collect and document their discoveries. They bring back what they find for scientists to study. Around 90% of the world's caves remain unexplored and new species are being discovered all the time.

Trapped deep down in flooded cave systems, cut off from the outside world and with only a limited supply of food, you might think that life would be struggling to survive, but over millions of years animals have evolved that can make the most of these dark places. Creatures wait patiently to catch fellow cave residents as they swim by or gather microscopic food particles floating in the water that fills these underground labyrinths.

These animals, like the Mexican blind cave fish, evolved in total darkness so most of them have no eyes and no colour – what use would these be in the pitch black. Mexican tetra fish, living in rivers above ground, became trapped and isolated in an underground system of lakes when the water levels dropped. Over time they evolved into the subspecies of Mexican blind cave fish. The fish have extreme sensitivity to pressure and vibration as well as an acute sense of smell to compensate for their lack of vision. As there is no night or day inside the cave, their body clock is constantly 'awake', which means they never sleep and are always active. Their bodies are covered in sensory hair cells that respond to vibrations in the water and they swim towards any vibration they feel. Chemosensors around their mouths detect particles of food, such as guano, in the water that flows through the caves. They swim constantly, never sleep and are very solitary.

Animals living in the extreme environments inside caves have evolved amazing senses that mean they are able to reproduce, find a tasty meal and avoid being eaten in the dark. Some have chemosensors that work like taste and smell, enabling them to detect microscopic bits of food in the water. Others have antennae and modified legs covered with mechanosensors that help them to sense the presence of other animals by picking up movements or changes in pressure. One unusual species has even evolved the ability to find its prey by sensing its electrical field – known as electrosensing.

HERALD MOTH
Scoliopteryx libatrix
Europe and North America

To avoid freezing in the cold
winter months the herald moth
hibernates in caves. Hiding in
cracks in the rock allows the
moth to remain at a stable
temperature in the sheltered
cave environment.

CAVE SWIFTLET
Collocalia sp.
Malaysia

These swiftlets nest inside caves at night because they offer safety from predators. Returning every evening, each swiftlet must echolocate to find its nest amongst the thousands or even millions of others inside the cave.

GIANT CENTIPEDE
Scolopendra gigantea
Venezuela

These giant centipedes aren't interested in eating the cockroaches scurrying around the cave floor. They're after something bigger – bats. Hanging from the cave walls they pounce on passing bats, injecting them with venom before devouring them.

JUVENILE AFRICAN DWARF CROCODILE
Osteolaemus tetraspis
Abanda cave system, Gabon

These are the only crocodiles in the world known to spend most of their lives in caves – the females will only leave to nest and lay their eggs in the surrounding forest. The bat-filled tunnels keep them well fed and provide shelter but with an unexpected consequence – the chemistry of the guano (bat poo) that accumulates inside the caves turns their scales orange.

GIANT CAVE COCKROACH
Blaberus giganteus
Central America and northern South America

If you went into a cave in Central America, you would likely see huge mounds of guano (bat poo) covered with feasting cockroaches. The flat body shape of the giant cave cockroach means that, despite being one of the largest cockroaches in the world, it can squeeze into nooks and crannies to hide from predators.

PUERTO RICAN CAVE BOA
Chilabothrus inornatus
Puerto Rico

Imagine climbing into a cave, looking up and seeing the ceiling covered with snakes! These boas hang from the cave roof to catch bats as they fly in and out. Once a boa has caught a bat it will squeeze it to death.

GALATHEID CRAB
Munidopsis polymorpha
**Jameos del Agua cave
system, Lanzarote,
Canary Islands**

Found only in the flooded
marine caves of the Canary
Islands, this blind, white crab
uses touch and smell to find
food carried in by the sea. Its
closest relatives live in the dark
ocean depths.

REMIPEDE
Xibalbanus tulumensis
Cenote Crustacea,
Yucatan Peninsula, Mexico

Discovered in 1981, remipedes
are the only venomous
crustaceans in the world. Using
their antennae they detect the
movements and chemicals
produced by shrimp before
immobilising them with their
venom.

OLM
Proteus anguinus
Dinaric Alps,
south eastern Europe

Unlike most amphibians, these salamanders eat, sleep and breed in water. By detecting the electrical fields of objects in their environment they can sense cave walls, tasty snails and other olms in the dark. In the past, people used to think olms were baby dragons.

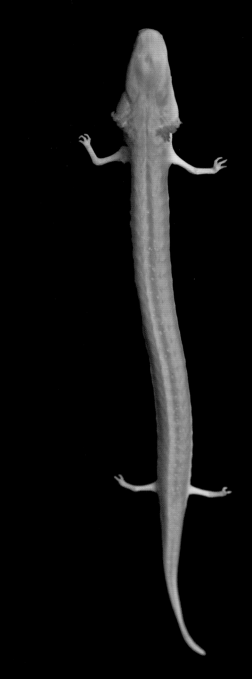

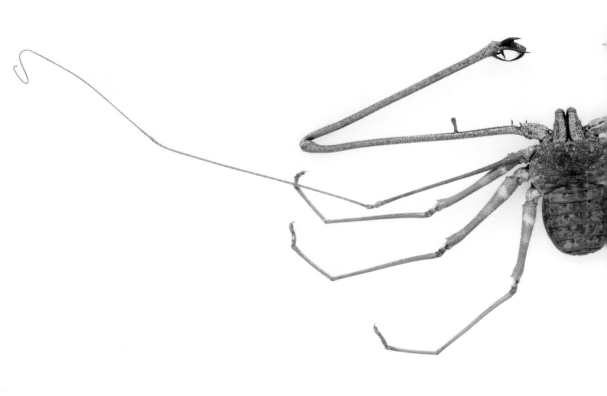

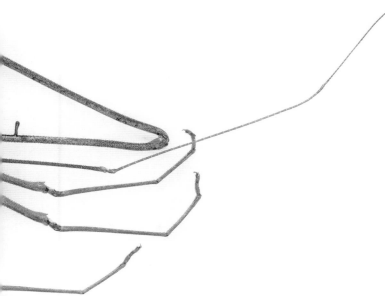

WHIP SPIDER
Euphrynichus bacillifer
Mozambique

Look how long this whip spider's second pair of legs is. Lying in wait, it uses these like antennae to sense the surrounding environment. These legs are covered in mechanosensors that pick up movements in the air, alerting the whip spider to the presence of a potential meal.

Life in the
deep

Dive beneath the waves and sink down to the deep, dark depths of the ocean. Down here tentacled creatures drift in the dark, fish scavenge for food and mysterious lights flash in the distance. Even in this vast watery realm where sunlight never reaches, life still flourishes.

The ocean is the largest habitat on Earth – and most of it is dark. Beyond a depth of 1,000 metres sunlight disappears and darkness, crushing pressure and low temperatures are the norm. But even in these extreme conditions there is life. Animals scavenge for food and hunt prey in the sediment of the seafloor and in the open ocean. In areas of volcanic activity, hydrothermal vents occur, churning out chemical-rich liquid that provides energy for a whole host of deep-sea creatures. Only around 5% of the ocean has been explored, so there is still much to be discovered.

Across the cold expanse of the seabed, small pockets of abundant life can be found thriving around hydrothermal vents. These chimneys spew out sulphurous liquids often hotter than 400°C from deep beneath the Earth's crust. The vents produce chemicals that provide a source of energy for a host of microbes that in turn provide food for the whole ecosystem, from tube worms and shrimp to crabs and sharks.

In water, the deeper you go, the darker it gets. By the time you reach a depth of 1,000 metres all sunlight has been absorbed – everything living deeper than this has to be able to survive in near darkness. Like animals in caves, those in the deep sea have evolved enhanced senses that enable them to find food, search for mates and avoid predators in this environment. Some animals use chemosensors to detect the scent of a rotting whale carcass from miles away by the tiny particles that drift in the current. Others use mechanosensors to sense the movements in the water created by animals swimming by, enabling them to detect the presence of predators and prey.

Unlike many cave creatures, most animals in the deep sea have eyes, but if there's no sunlight down there then why do they need them? In the deep sea an astonishing 90% of animals make their own light, a phenomenon known as bioluminescence. Through the gloom, blue light twinkles, green mucus glows and red lights flash. Deep-sea creatures can use light to illuminate or stun prey and also to communicate with each other. Glowing lights camouflage while a flash might scare away a predator or create a distraction. In the dark depths, producing light is a key survival strategy.

Without light from the Sun to provide energy, food is limited in the dark depths of the ocean. Many deep-sea animals are scavengers, surviving off small bits of decaying plants and animals that drift down from above – known as marine snow. But there are also predators in the depths. They use light to help capture their prey. Some use glowing light to lure unsuspecting animals towards their jaws, others use it to disguise themselves or to mask the shape of their bodies. Swim towards an innocent-looking light in the deep sea and it might be the last thing you do.

In thousands of miles of dark open ocean how do you find each other? Some animals produce glowing patterns of light to recognise one another and to signal to potential mates. But making yourself too obvious comes with a risk – your date might become someone else's dinner. A few species use yellow or red light because most deep-sea creatures can't see these colours, allowing them to attract a mate without drawing attention to themselves.

Over millions of years, animals have evolved numerous different strategies to defend themselves, and using light can be one of the most spectacular there is. A sudden flash can startle or blind a predator, glowing lights can act as a distraction or a swirl of bright blue can be an alarm call. Under the cover of light they escape and swim safely away, retreating back into the dark.

Little sunlight reaches the twilight zone, 200–1,000 metres deep. It's just bright enough for large-eyed creatures to spot the silhouette of a predator or prey against the background of light from the surface. So how do you stay hidden in the open ocean? Camouflage is key to survival and surprisingly making light could actually help you hide. Many deep-sea creatures use bioluminescent organs called photophores to create patterns of light on their bodies. These patterns break up their outlines, making them harder to spot against the light from above. This counter-illumination helps them to hide in plain sight.

An entire microscopic ecosystem floats in the ocean currents. Each evening, as the Sun goes down, the greatest migration on the planet takes place as billions of deep-sea animals rise up from the watery depths to feed. In the well-lit surface waters microscopic plants called phytoplankton get energy from the Sun. As darkness descends tiny animals known as zooplankton migrate up from the depths of the ocean to eat the phytoplankton. Larger predators, such as fish and squid, follow to feed on the zooplankton. The feeding frenzy continues until dawn. But as soon as the Sun rises, these animals descend back to the relative safety of the darkness below.

SEA CUCUMBER
Oneirophanta mutabilis
Worldwide
Depth: 2,500–6,000 metres

With peg-like feet and sensory tentacles, sea cucumbers crawl along the seafloor sucking up anything edible they find. They are one of the most common animals on the abyssal plains – the vast stretches of sediment kilometres below the surface of the ocean.

SEA SPIDER
Decolopoda australis
Antarctica
Depth: 50–1,900 metres

There's not much food in the darkness underneath the Antarctic ice, but these sea spiders can still grow up to 76 centimetres from claw to claw. They travel across the seafloor looking for slow-moving or stationary animals, such as sponges, to eat.

'DISCOVERY' EXPEDITI
St. 42   Date 1·IV·26
Net OTL   Depth of Net

GIANT ISOPOD
Bathynomus giganteus
Atlantic Ocean
Depth: 310–2,140 metres

The giant isopod is an ocean-dwelling relative of the woodlouse with large, reflective eyes. As a scavenger it eats anything it comes across on the seafloor, from dead seals to sea cucumbers.

DUMBO OCTOPUS
Cirroteuthis sp.
**North Atlantic Ocean and
North Pacific Ocean
Depth: 700–5,000 metres**

One of the largest animals
in the deep sea, the Dumbo
octopus can grow up to
1.5 metres in length. As it
swims along, its large fins look
like ears, earning it the name
Dumbo.

BLIND VENT CRAB
Bythograea thermydron
East Pacific Rise vent systems in the Pacific Ocean
Depth: 2,500 metres

Despite what their name suggests blind vent crabs aren't actually blind – they just see differently. Instead of eyes they have naked retinas that enable them to see infra-red light. This means they can see hydrothermal vents by the heat they give off.

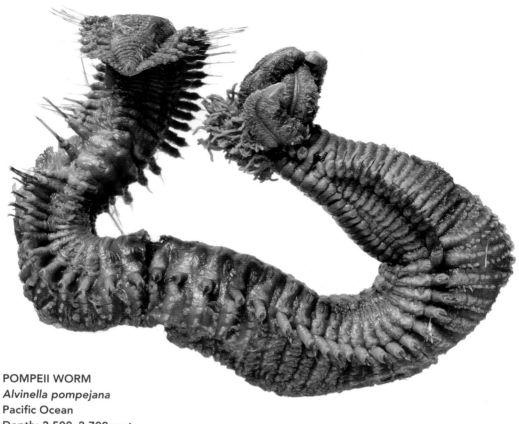

POMPEII WORM
Alvinella pompejana
Pacific Ocean
Depth: 2,500–2,700 metres

Imagine having your head in the fridge and your feet in the oven. Pompeii worms live with their tails attached to the hydrothermal vent surrounded by water as hot as 80°C and their heads surrounded by water that is a cooler 22°C. Scientists don't know how they survive in this heat.

BLIND VENT SHRIMP
Rimicaris kairei
Indian Ocean
Depth: 2,415–3,320 metres

Instead of eyes, these shrimp
have an area on their backs
that contains rhodopsin – the
pigment we use to see in low
light. This allows them to sense
and avoid the hottest areas of
the vent while feeding on the
bacteria that live there.

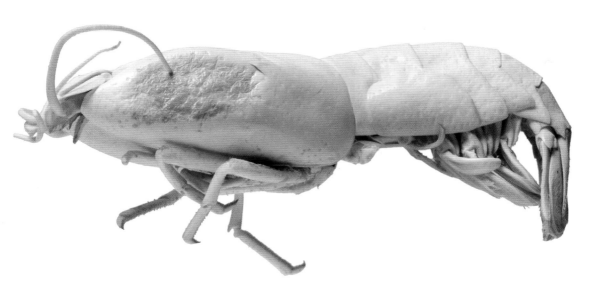

GIANT RED SHRIMP
Neognathophausia ingens
Worldwide
Depth: 250–4,000 metres

This shrimp can grow up to
35 centimetres in length.
Can you see its long
antennae? They are covered
with mechanosensors and
chemosensors for finding food.
In life this shrimp is dark red,
making it hard to spot in the
deep ocean, as red light is
absorbed quickly by water.

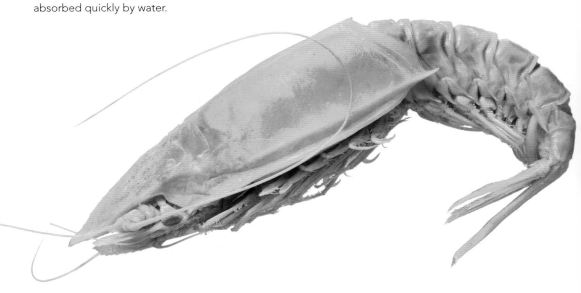

FEMALE SEADEVIL
Melanocetus johnsonii
Worldwide
Depth: 100–4,500 metres

It can be difficult to find a mate in the vast ocean. Female seadevils release pheromones to attract a mate. When a male finally finds a female he attaches himself to her like a parasite, obtaining all his nutrients from her blood.

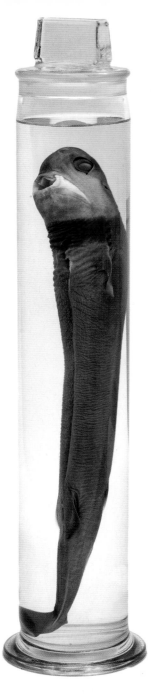

COOKIE CUTTER SHARK
Isistius brasiliensis
Atlantic Ocean, Pacific Ocean
and Indian Ocean
Depth: 0–3,500 metres

Scientists think the bioluminescent pattern on this shark's belly helps make the dark patch on its neck look like a smaller fish to those viewing it from below. Fish approach the shark in pursuit of an easy catch, but once they're within striking distance the cookie cutter shark, living up to its name, takes a circular chunk out of them.

SLOANE'S VIPERFISH
Chauliodus sloani
Worldwide
Depth: 200–2,000 metres

Light organs on its belly
camouflage the viperfish,
while a light on the end of
its long dorsal fin lures prey
close enough to be attacked.
The viperfish has the biggest
teeth relative to the size of its
body of any fish in the sea. Its
teeth are so big that when the
viperfish shuts its mouth the
bottom teeth slide up the front
of its face!

FOOTBALL FISH
Himantolophus groenlandicus
Worldwide
Depth: 300–3,000 metres

The football fish can move its flashing bioluminescent lure around above its head to attract unsuspecting prey towards it in the dark. This species was discovered in 1837 and was the first deep-sea angler fish ever to be described.

STOPLIGHT LOOSEJAW
Malacosteus niger
Worldwide
Depth: 500–4,000 metres

Stoplight loosejaws have an advantage – they can see red light in the ocean, which is invisible to most deep-sea life. They have red bioluminescent headlights, as well as blue photophores, so they can look for food and find a mate without being seen themselves.

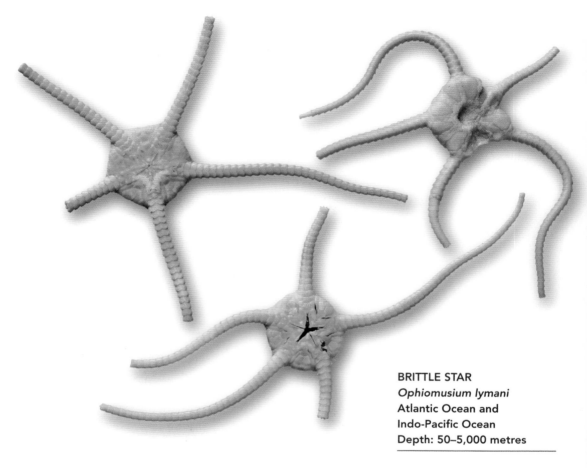

BRITTLE STAR
Ophiomusium lymani
**Atlantic Ocean and
Indo-Pacific Ocean
Depth: 50–5,000 metres**

Brittle stars have evolved
a whole armoury of
bioluminescent defensive
tools. When approached
some species flash brightly to
temporarily blind predators.
Others produce gently
glowing, foul-tasting mucus
to signal that they are toxic.

SEA-LILY
Neocrinus decorus
Caribbean Sea
Depth: 150–1,200 metres

Although they look like plants, sea-lilies are actually animals related to starfish. Some sea-lilies create flashes of light that travel along their bodies to scare away anything that might eat them.

KRILL
Euphausiids
Worldwide
Depth: 0– 2,000 metres

These small shrimp-like
creatures are top of the
menu for many predators.
To avoid being eaten they
have bioluminescent bellies
for camouflage and some can
even spit out glowing gloop
when threatened – a bright
smoke screen to hide their
escape.

VELVET BELLY LANTERNSHARK
Etmopterus spinax
Atlantic Ocean and the Mediterranean Sea
Depth: 200–2,500 metres

One of the smallest and most common sharks in the ocean, the velvet belly lanternshark has many predators, including the gulper shark. It disguises its silhouette with photophores covering its belly that match the light coming down through the water from above.

The Natural History Museum
looks after a world-class collection
of over 80 million specimens. It
is also a leading scientific research
institution, with ground-breaking
projects in more than 68 countries.
About 200 scientists work at the
Museum, researching the valuable
collections to better understand
life on Earth. Every year more than
five million visitors, of all ages and
levels of interest, are welcomed
through the Museum's doors.

First published by the Natural History Museum,
Cromwell Road, London SW7 5BD

ISBN 978 0565 094010

A catalogue record for this book is available from
the British Library

10 9 8 7 6 5 4 3 2 1

Designed by Bobby Birchall, Bobby&Co.
Reproduction by Saxon Digital Services UK
Printed by Toppan Leefung Printing Limited, China

Front cover: Spectral Tarsier (*Tarsius tarsier*)
© Quentin Martinez/Getty Images
Back cover: Male Atlas moth, *Attacus atlas*

What are Deserts?

Deserts are dry places. They usually get less than 250 millimetres of rain or snow each year.

There are two main types of desert – hot and cold.

Hot deserts have lots of sand or rock and very high temperatures in summer. Hot deserts are usually at low **elevations**. The air is very dry and there are few clouds. This can cause the temperature to drop below freezing point at night.

Cold deserts have sand, rocks and ice. They are usually at high elevations, such as on **plateaux**. It is cooler at high elevations, especially in winter. Antarctica is an example of a cold desert. Instead of raining, it often snows in cold deserts.

The barrel cactus stores water.

GO FACTS **NATURAL ENVIRONMENTS**

Deserts

A & C BLACK · LONDON

Deserts

contents

Hardback edition
ISBN 978-1-4081-0489-7

Paperback edition
ISBN 978-1-4081-0488-0

A CIP record for this book is available from the British Library.

Author: Ian Rohr
Publisher: Katy Pike
Editor: Mark Stafford
Design and layout by The Modern Art Production Group

Image credits: p19 (all)–Mark Stafford
Printed in China by WKT Company Ltd.

This publication is produced using paper that is made from wood grown in
managed sustainable forests. It is natural, renewable and recyclable. The
logging and manufacturing processes conform to the environmental regulations
of the country of origin.

Australian deserts are hot deserts.

The Gobi Desert in Mongolia is a cold desert.

GO FACT!

HOTTEST AND COLDEST

The highest recorded temperature on Earth was 57.7 °C (135.9 °F) in Libya. The lowest temperature was −89.2 °C (-128.6 °F) in Antarctica.

Antarctica is the driest continent on Earth.

5

Deserts of the World

Each desert is different, but they all have some common features.

What a desert looks like depends on **erosion**. This is the effect of wind and water on rock. It doesn't rain much in the desert. When it does rain, it is often during storms. The rain quickly erodes rocks. Wind also erodes rocks, but it does this slowly and constantly.

Soft rocks are eroded to fine grains of sand. Winds push the sand into sand dunes. Wind storms can carry sand dunes over great distances.

Hard rocks are eroded to stones and pebbles. Nearly half of the world's deserts are plains covered with rocks and pebbles. Only 20 per cent of deserts are covered in sand.

The blue-tongued lizard lives in Australian deserts and forests.

DID YOU KNOW?

Sand dunes can sing! Some sand dunes make a loud, low rumble, even if there is no wind blowing. The sound is caused by sand sliding down the steep sides of dunes.

These rock formations in Monument Valley, USA, were created by erosion.

Kata Tjuta in Australia's Central Desert was formed by the erosion of mountains.

Sand dunes can reach 400 metres high.

Although deserts are dry, you can still find water in them.

Some deserts have rivers and oases.

The Nile and Colorado Rivers run through deserts. The soil soaks up some water from the rivers, and the hot weather causes a lot of water to **evaporate**.

An oasis is a place where there is a reliable water supply. An oasis forms where underground water comes to the desert surface as a **spring**. People can make oases by digging wells.

Deserts of the World

1 Antarctic Desert
2 Arabian Desert
3 Atacama Desert
4 Chihuahuan Desert
5 Gibson Desert
6 Gobi Desert
7 Great Basin Desert
8 Great Sandy Desert
9 Great Victoria Desert
10 Dasht-e Kavir Desert
11 Kalahari Desert
12 Mojave Desert
13 Namib Desert
14 Sahara Desert
15 Sonoran Desert
16 Takla Makan Desert

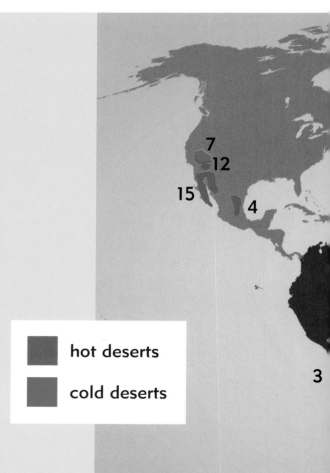

■ hot deserts
■ cold deserts

Desert lakes often dry out.

9

The Sahara

The Sahara is the largest hot desert on Earth. It covers one-third of Africa.

About one-quarter of the Sahara is made up of sand dunes and rocky plateaux. The rest of the desert is made up of gravel plains.

Plants, animals and millions of people live in the Sahara. It can get hotter than 50 °C (122 °F). The Sahara gets only 80 millimetres of rain each year. Violent sand and dust storms can blow for days. These make travel in the desert dangerous.

The Sahara has many oases, but there are long distances between them. People would not be able to live in the Sahara without oases.

Arabian camel with a decorative saddle

Some people who live in the Sahara are **nomads**.

Date palms grow at oases.

A headdress protects people from cold and blowing sand.

"Sahara" comes from the Arabic word for desert.

Desert Plants

Desert plants have special features that allow them to collect, store and conserve water.

Some desert plants have roots that cover a wide area, just below the ground. Other plants have roots that go deep underground. Mosses and lichens get water, such as **dew**, from above the ground.

prickly pear leaves

Many desert plants store water in their hollow leaves, stems or roots. These plants are called **succulents**. Plants with thick skin, and with leaves that are small or like needles, don't lose the water that they store.

Some desert plants only grow and flower after the rain falls. Seeds lying on the ground for years begin to grow when it rains. Dry grasses may look dead above ground, but their roots remain alive underground.

12

A saguaro cactus can grow 20 metres tall.

The spikes on a cactus prevent animals from eating the plant.

GO FACTS

GREATEST VARIETY

The Sonoran Desert in the USA has more types of plant than any other desert in the world.

Aloe vera is a succulent.

The boab tree stores water in its trunk.

13

Desert Animals

Desert animals conserve water. They try to avoid very hot and very cold temperatures.

Animals get most of their water from the plants or animals they eat.

Reptiles store water and fat in their bodies. The Gila monster and Egyptian spiny tailed lizard save fat in their large tails. More than 100 reptile species live in the Sahara.

The fur or hair of large desert animals keeps them cool. The outer layer of a camel's coat can be 30 °C (86 °F) hotter than its body.

Some desert animals, such as the marsupial mole, burrow underground to escape extreme temperatures. It is cooler underground in hot deserts. In cold deserts, it is warmer underground.

Many hot desert animals are **nocturnal**. The addax, a nocturnal African antelope, digs a hole with its hooves and lies down in it during the hottest part of the day.

Geckos are nocturnal.

14

Penguins are desert animals.

Some desert birds, such as this roadrunner, cannot fly.

GO FACT!

THE LARGEST
The largest scorpion in the world is the emperor scorpion from Western Africa. It can grow more than 20 centimetres long and is a popular pet.

The thorny devil drinks the dew that collects on its back.

15

A Desert Food Chain

Some desert animals eat plants. Some desert animals eat other animals.

Many desert animals are both **predators** and **prey**. Survival depends on catching food but not being caught.

1. Plants make their own food from the energy of the Sun.

2. Small animals and insects eat the seeds, leaves and flowers of these plants.

3. Small predators eat the plant eaters and other small predators.

4. Large predators eat smaller predators and plant eaters.

Desert animals are often the same colour as the ground, so predators can't see them.

Prickly pear

Jack rabbit

Golden eagle

Rattlesnake

1 → 2

4 ← 3

17

Staying Cool

In a hot desert, animals stay cool underground. The soil acts as an **insulator**.

An insulator slows down or stops the movement of heat. Test for yourself how well soil works as an insulator.

What you need:

- two large tin cans
- two small tin cans
- two thermometers
- soil
- warm water
- a watch or clock
- pen and paper

Desert tortoises dig deep burrows to keep cool during the day and warm at night.

18

1 Put warm water and a thermometer in each of the small cans.

2 Place each small can inside a large can.

soil

4 Write down the temperature of each of the thermometers. Repeat this every five minutes for 30 minutes. What is happening to the temperatures?

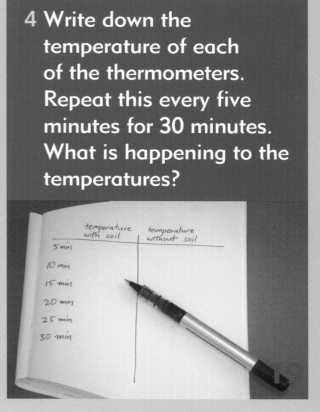

3 Fill around ONE of the small cans with soil.

Threats to Deserts

Deserts are easily damaged. Mining and farms are the biggest threat to deserts.

Deserts often contain oil and iron ore. Drilling for oil and mining can harm desert environments.

Tourists can damage desert water supplies. Vehicles damage desert soils and plants.

When farms are on the edge of a desert, they can damage the fragile desert soil.

Farm animals pound the soil with their hooves. This breaks up the soil. It is then more likely to be eroded by wind and rain. When people collect firewood, or graze farm animals, they reduce the number of plants that help to bind the soil.

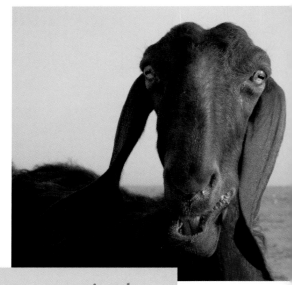

Goats are raised in African deserts.

The oryx antelope has been hunted to the edge of extinction.

There are many oil wells and refineries in the deserts of the Middle East.

THE HIGHEST
The highest desert in the world is the Qaidam Depression in China. It is 2600 metres above sea level.

Deserts are popular places to visit.

Some people treat deserts like rubbish dumps.

Desert Features

Rock		
mesa (rhymes with "blazer")	a large, isolated flat-topped rock	
butte (rhymes with "mute")	a hill like a mesa, but with steeper sides	
Sand		
erg (rhymes with "iceberg")	a large area of moving sand dunes	
barchan (rhymes with "barn")	a sand dune with a curved ridge	

Glossary

dew	drops of water that form on the ground during the night
elevation	height of land above the level of the sea
erosion	breaking down rock by wind and water
evaporate	to change from a liquid or solid to a gas
insulator	a material that electricity, heat or sound cannot go through
nocturnal	active during the night
nomad	a person who moves around rather than living in one place
plateau	a large, flat area of land, high above sea level
predator	an animal that hunts, kills and eats other animals
prey	an animal that is hunted and killed by another animal
spring	a place where water naturally flows from the ground
succulent	a plant that stores water in its leaves and stem

Index